7 Steps for Finding and Preparing for Networking Events

Michelle A. Roberts, M.A.

ISBN:1499182503
ISBN-13:9781499182507

DEDICATION

I want to thank my Abba Father for Life, Health, Strength, Faithfulness and Favor over my Life! Without Him I would be nothing!

I also want to Thank my Dedicated Readers and Followers.

CONTENTS

Michelle A. Roberts, M.A.

ACKNOWLEDGMENTS

Special Thanks to my tribe: My Mother, Elease J. Walker, Grandmother Mary Lee Tyler, sisters LaTonya Denise Walker and Keisha Nicolle Walker, My children Jason Roberts, Mariah Roberts and Essence Roberts and my little Nephew Kason Brunson. I love you so much, thanks for always having my back.

INTRODUCTION

Finding and Preparing for a Networking event as a Vendor can be daunting but these 7 practical steps will give you an easy "how to" introduction to help you be successful in finding a networking opportunity and presenting as a Vendor.

I. **Determine Your Target Market**

Are you going to Target Everybody? Or do you want to specialize? It's best in my opinion to have a target audience and go from there. If you are just getting started of course, don't turn down any business and as you go along you will develop and determine your niche. Some examples of vendor specialized areas to consider are as follows:

NOTE: *Since I specialize in the travel industry the following examples or for the travel Industry. If you are in another industry, you will have to determine your target market depending on your industry and your business goals for being a Vendor.*

Cruisers (*i.e. Carnival, Royal Caribbean, Norwegian Cruise Line, River Cruises, Crystal and Princess, Disney i.e. you may just want to major on one particular cruise line specifically*)

Brides/Grooms/Honeymooners (*couples or individual planning for marriage or honeymoon destination*)

Senior Citizens (*age group of 55 and older*)

Special needs (*any person traveling with a disability or limited mobility*)

Sports Fans (*professional football trips, college football, basketball, final four, SEC, golfers, bowlers, horse shoes, and Olympics, etc.*)

Casino trips (*groups or individual who like to gamble i.e. Las Vegas, Cherokee Casinos, and Dog Racing etc.*)

Family Vacations (*This can be Mom, Dad and Children, single parents and children, grandparents and grandchildren, family reunions these may be spring break vacations, summer vacations, Christmas holiday or Thanksgiving trips etc.*)

Singles (*unmarried couples, friends, girlfriend trips, all male trips (golfing, fishing, games, Dominican Republic, etc.*)

LGBT Community (*i.e. Lesbian, Gay, Bisexual and Transgender is a growing market*)

Associations (ABWA, National Tax Association, Sororities, Fraternities etc.)

II. Determine your Budget for events

A. If you are just starting out in business, you may have a limited budget. As a novice, you should look for those free or low cost events. If you are more established and have more advertising dollars, your budget for events will provide more visibility and opportunity for branding to future customers or partners in networking.

Advantages of having a partner are:

1. You will consider events you can dominate as a team and split the cost between team members and

2. You can divide any leads received between partners / team members.

B. Some events are free if you sponsor a gift i.e. 3 day 2

night hotel stay, gas card, gift card etc.

C. Events may vary in price. I have seen as low as $25.00 and as high as $1500.00 depending on the event i.e. Networking events may be a range of $50.00 to $200 depending upon placement of table at the event. Hair shows i.e. Bronner Brothers, Natural Hair events, etc. that expects 10,000 or more in attendee traffic can start at or around $800 for vending tables. So you see the wide disparity in price.

III. Where do you Find Vending / Event opportunities

A. There are several sources for finding vending opportunities that are listed below. In addition to the sources provided, also take advantage of networking with other vendors. Consider partnering for event as a tradeoff exchanging opportunities with other vendors and they in turn will share opportunities with you in the future. When in attendance at all events and networking sessions, always exchange cards with the audience and especially other vendors at these events.

1. Google Search (networking events in your city)
2. Look for Out Door Festivals
3. Meet up.com

4. Eventbrite.com

5. Job Fairs

6. Facebook (search for networking events, job fairs and vendor opportunities) There are endless results on Facebook so narrow down your search to your city and surrounding areas.

IV. Get your Collateral/Material

1. If you are promoting a particular service or you are a direct seller then have your literature, cd, books or flyers to give away. If you have to purchase these items make sure this is a part of your budget.

2. Vendors, love to give a way collateral! Call, email, and go to the website of vendors whose material you are interested in having i.e. books, pens, and pads, bags, posters and signs. Then, order free materials. Because quantities vary per vendor and you are having a big event, you will most likely have to call those vendors you have

targeted to get larger quantities. Don't worry! It will be free. For Example, I specialize in Travel. Here are some of the vendors I have contacted:

3. Sandals contact the BDM (Business Development Manager) in your area or go to website

4. Apple Vacations

5. GoGo Vacations

6. Cruise lines i.e. Carnival, Royal Caribbean, Norwegian Cruise Line, Princess, Crystal, Cunard, Viking River Cruise etc.

7. Disney

8. Hotels (*Marriott, Hilton, Hyatt etc.*)

v. **Prepare for Event**

A. Just as finding an event is important, being properly prepared is key. Most events have an estimated amount of people they are expecting, based upon that estimate i.e. 200 guests or 3,000 guests. You will need enough materials for the event. Your tables should look as professional as possible. You MUST calculate your budget wisely if you are new in the business and determine the most effective areas for use. Some of those areas are as follows:

B. Personalized Banner or Sign (I have used Vista print and local printing companies)

C. Business Cards, Informational Cards, Posters

D. Table Cloth

E. Plastic Display containers for Books and

Literature, (Needs to look neat and professional)

you can find these at dollar store and office

supply stores

F. Booth Forms (this should contain the information

you want to collect i.e. Name, email, phone

number and questions relevant to your

networking effort.) Sample Booth Forms or in

Appendix

G. Pens

H. Candy (optional)

I. Give away (optional) I use this all the time 3 day 2

night vacation (Grand Incentives) or

Restaurant.com gift card. (Very effective)

vi. Practice what you will say

A. This will need to be tailored to the event you are attending. For example, if it's a Networking event are you trying to recruit team mates or promote travel? Or if it's a bridal show are you looking to book honeymoon or destination weddings?   If you are frequenting job fairs because you are looking for sharp individuals to join our team, know what you want to say. If you have informational cards or literature for upcoming meetings, teleconferences, or webinars give that out as well at all of your networking events.

Example for job fair: We are looking for people who are absolutely serious about building a business and making money from home. So *"Prospects Name"*, how serious are you about starting a home business? Tell me why.

Great! Let me tell you about the company I work with.

Bridal show: Getting married is so exciting! We help to take the stress out of planning your honey moon or destination wedding. We believe in making it all about you. What's your dream destination and budget?

VII.   Next Day-Follow up

A. Organize your leads

B. Separate into Business opportunity and Travel

accommodations

C. Schedule time for follow up and research

D. Look for next Event

VIII. Conclusion

A. The 7 steps to Prepare for your Networking Event as a Travel Vendor

B. Determine Your Target Market

C. Determine your Budget

D. Find your Event

E. Get your Collateral

F. Prepare for Event

G. Practice what you Will Say

H. Follow up on Leads

Following these steps will impact your event and help you take your business to the next level. You will get the numbers generated in leads and you will begin to significantly increase your networking capabilities and determine a niche market.

ABOUT THE AUTHOR

Michelle A. Roberts, M.A., Author, Speaker, Entrepreneur

Challenge Conqueror

Michelle encourages Woman that they are overcomers and can comeback from any challenge.

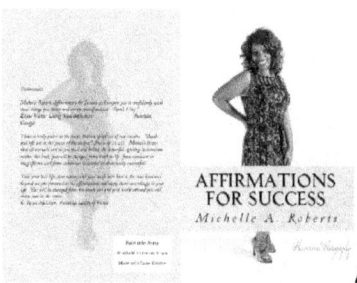

Author of Affirmations for Success

Her topics include:

- **The Power is in Your Mouth**
- **Divorce is not a Destroyer**
- **Winning the battle over weight**
- **Why you have Such a Pretty Face is not a Compliment**
- **Single Moms are Winners**
- **The Power of Owning your Own Business**

Michelle Roberts is a fighter and a winner after being married for 17 years I finally came to myself and realized that my drug addicted husband would not change. See I was not raised with my father and always longed for that relationship so I stayed to LONG. I was so depressed I was now carrying 268lbs on 5 foot frame. I thought no one would want a fat girl with 3 babies. I finally took charge of my life. I had life altering surgery gastric by-pass I loss over 110 lbs. Got a divorce, Went back to school and completed a BSM and MA now 2 classes away from starting my Dissertation for my Doctorate. Yes it was hard, yes I cried, yes I complained some times. But I looked at my 3 children and a fight for dear life rose in me.

I am now a proud owner of a Roberts Travel Services and Executive Director of a Non Profit, Harvest Nets Enterprises, which helps to feed over 5000 children every summer. I also meet monthly with other Women entrepreneurs, both inspiring and established through Xperience Connections where our mission is to encourage and facilitate the growth, performance and integrity of professional women by creating opportunities to foster relationships through a creative exchange of information and referrals. I have 2 children in college, and one child who has completed 2 years of college and now is seeking entry into the military.

And what did I learn? I know that Life can begin again after Tragedy. Do you ever feel like Giving up? Everyone has felt this way at some point or

another, why because life has a way of knocking the
wind out of you. Everyone's path is different. What
effects one person may not bother the other one in
the same way; Strength in different situations comes
in different doses. But hold on to the fact that
Destiny is calling you and you must be prepared to
answer and be in position to collide with it.

Contact: Michelle A. Roberts

404-935-8113

http://about.me/michellearobertsllc

michelleantoinetteroberts@gmail.com

www.facebook.com/michellearobertsinc

www.robertstourismservices.com